Every love story is beautiful but ours is my favorite

Copyright © 2025 by Annette Bridges

www.annettebridges.com

Published by Ranch House Press

All rights reserved. Except as permitted under the U.S. Copyright Ac t of 1976, no part of this publication may be reproduced, distributed, or transmitted in any form or by any means, or stored in a database or retrieval system, without the prior written permision of the author.

Poem written by Annette Bridges.
Original doodle illustrations drawn by the author.

Designed by Janie Owen-Bugh
www.janieowenbugh.com

Printed in the United States of America.

ISBN 978-1-946371-53-9

I've loved kissing you from the start.

I'm happy by your side anywhere we go.

You and me...
my favorite duo.

Making memories is always better with you.

You are my soulmate and my dream come true.

You are my everything, my home is where you are.

You are my sunshine, my moon beams and all my stars.

There's nothing I love more than laughing with you.

I love your hand in mine in whatever we do.

Love is weathering the storms of life together.

You are my forever sweetheart forever.

I want to dance with only you ~
from the moment we met, I knew.

P.S. I love you, too!

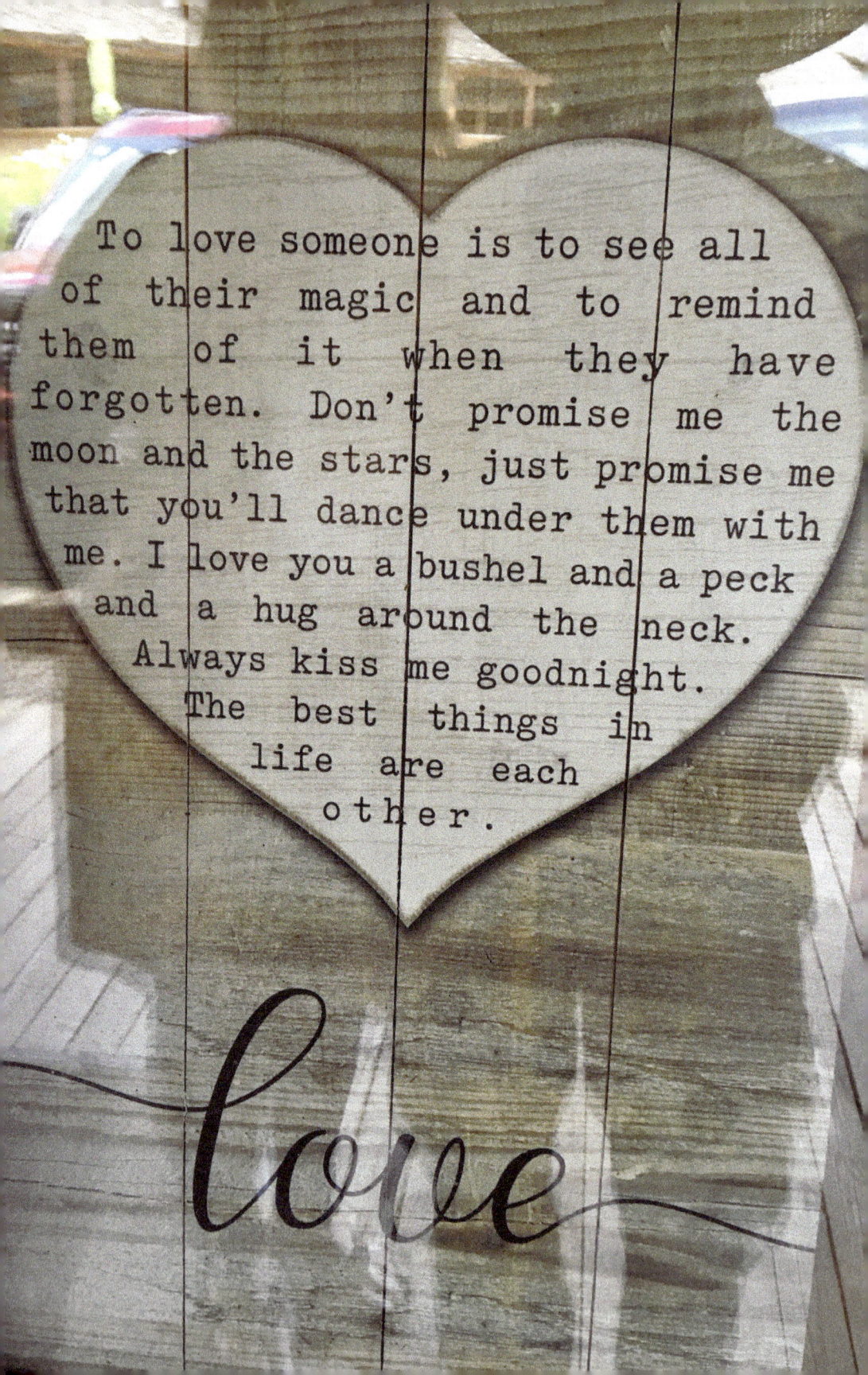

About the Author

Annette Bridges and her husband John are Texas cattle ranchers and have been married over forty years. Annette writes a monthly column in North Texas Farm & Ranch magazine titled, "When a city girl goes country." And she's the founder of Ranch House Press & Gifts.

She's written books and created journals, coloring and cookbooks especially tailored for women, children as well as cow, dachshund and cat lovers. She loves to write, doodle, paint and take photos of her animal friends. She uses her art and photography to create all kinds of products you'll find in her shop.

This is a photograph showing the reflection of Annette and her hubby looking in a shop window at one of their favorite Colorado mountain towns. They both loved this window sign and totally agree with its message. They share it here as good advice for every love story.

You can learn more about Annette and read all of her magazine columns on her website at annettebridges.com. You can learn more about her Ranch House Gift Shop, too!

Titles by Annette Bridges

Books:

Our Love Story
A gift book of playful doodles with messages for the love of your life

When Cattitude Meets Coffee
Playful quotes for coffee lovers

Mamma Said So
20 Pearls of Wisdom from a Southern Sage

101 Things Women Want from Their Men
Written collectively by hundreds of women who shared their advice

A Dachshund Tale
Lessons learned from my dog

Oh, How the Years Fly By!
A whimsical inspirational quote book

The Gospel According to Mamma
One mother's philosophy on love, God, money, aging, decisions, change, and much more

Be Queen of Your Life
A savvy mom helps daughters command and rule their lives

Have Lipstick, Will Travel
How to reimagine your life, purpose, and hair color

Adult Coloring Books:

Color-N-Doodle Your World
An inspiring collection of coloring pages with your own space to doodle and create

Oh, How the Years Fly By!
A whimsical adult coloring book

Journals & Planners:

Karma is a Cat Personal Planner
Monthly calendars, cat quotes and notes pages

Okay, We Grew Old Together... Now What?
A couple's journal

My Furry Friend
A keepsake journal

Anytime Journal
Because anytime is a good time to journal

Jot Journals
18 themed pocket-sized journals

Color Your World Journal Series
18 themed large journals

Books For Children:

Lady and Bella: Totally Different, Totally Friends
A coloring storybook for children

Totally Friends Journal
Especially for children

Totally different, Totally friends
Full-color hardcover storybook about friendship

Lady and Bella's Alphabet Kitchen Cookbook: A to Z Recipes for Kid Cooks
Full-color hardcover cookbook that provides first-time cooks with easy-to-follow yummy recipes and more

Order at bookstores, Amazon, and Annette's Etsy shop at etsy.com/shop/RanchHouseGiftShop.

www.ingramcontent.com/pod-product-compliance
Lightning Source LLC
Chambersburg PA
CBHW061806070526
44586CB00023B/2734